Raising Ducks Naturally:

Guide For Beginners On How To Raise

Healthy Ducks Without A Pond, How to

Feed Them, And Take Care for Them

Table of content

Introduction

If you've ever had a hankering to create your own small holding then the concept of chickens will undoubtedly have arisen.

But have you ever considered ducks? They can be raised alongside your chickens or you may just want to do it for fun. After all, ducks are adorable creatures!

It is worth noting that in most places there are no issues with keeping a few ducks but it is always worth checking with your local authority first. If you have close neighbors you may wish to speak to them as well.

Ducks will give you eggs on a regular basis. In fact you may be surprised to learn that the average duck will lay more eggs than a chicken each year. The eggs are bigger and they were set to be the biggest provider of eggs until it was discovered that chickens were very tolerant of intensive farming techniques.

There are several other benefits to keeping ducks as opposed to chickens. For example, ducks are great at getting rid of unwanted bugs in your yard but they will not scratch every piece of land into dusty soil and spread it across the garden path!

Ducks are also surprisingly easy to keep, a pond is not essential although you will need some water for them to sit in.

You will also need to consider what type of ducks you wish to keep. There are many different breeds to choose from and all have their own merits. However, the most popular ducks for at home are:

- **The Pekin**

This is the traditional white duck which comes from China and was originally used just for its meat. They are friendly, calm and cannot fly. They generally lay up to 200 eggs per year and make great pets!

- **Indian Runner**

These actually come from Indonesia and were used to control insects in the rice feeds. They are also very friendly but more easily spooked than the Pekin. Again you can expect up to 200 eggs per year!

- **Mallard**

These ducks are small and fly extremely well. If you want to keep them you're going to need a roof on their outside space.

These are the chattiest ducks on this list and are always full of energy. They will spend most of the day in the water if the opportunity arises.

The mallard is not as productive as the other ducks; you can expect up to 120 eggs a year from them.

- **Khaki Campbell**

This breed is a cross of the mallard, Rouen and the runner. It is the most successful duck at laying eggs with yields of up to 300 per year!

They are generally poor flyers so should stay close to your yard. They are friendly but again a little more nervous than the Pekin.

- **Swedish**

The Swedish duck originates from Pomerania and lays up to 180 eggs per year. It is a very pretty duck and able to survive in virtually all temperatures.

They are great for your back yard as they are friendly and very difficult to spook. As a heavy duck their flying ability s limited.

- **Saxony**

This is the heaviest duck on this list at up to 8 pounds. They have long legs and need some room to get around. You should see up to 200 eggs per year from one of these and they are very broody. This is good news if you're looking to have chicks!

You should be able to find these birds at most farms, hatcheries or even some stores. There are others, but these are generally regarded as the best options.

Chapter 1 – Creating The Right Habitat

Once you've decided on the right duck for your home then you need to create the right habitat to make them happy. This will help to ensure they produce eggs and don't make an excessive amount of noise.

It is important to be aware that the majority of domestic ducks can't fly. If you have one that can then you should consider clipping their wings. However, ducks are relatively easy prey for a number of animals and even some birds. This is why you need to create a secure habitat where they can go at night and when you're not able to keep an eye on them.

Here's what you need to consider and create to make the perfect habitat for your ducks, you and your neighbors:

Duck Numbers

The size of the pen you create will be dictated to some extent by the number of ducks you wish to keep.

Each duck needs enough space to preen themselves and walk round. Ideally this means giving each duck 4 square feet of space. Obviously you can go larger than the minimum amount but you should never go smaller.

If you want to keep four ducks then you need 16 square feet, that's only 4 feet by 4 feet!

Location

The next consideration is where you are going to put the ducks in your garden. They actually like human contact; if you want to interact with them then you're going to need to get easy access to them.

This may suggest them being near your house. However, you also need to consider your neighbors. While most ducks are fairly quiet the will make some noise. If your neighbors are likely to complain then you need to keep them as far away from their garden as possible.

Water

Ducks generally love water but you don't need to build a pond! The mallard will spend most of its time swimming and is perhaps not the best option if you don't have a pond.

The majority of the other duck breeds simply want somewhere to sit and preen while bathing.

This means that any container big enough for the ducks to sit in will suffice. The advantage of this over a pond is that you can easily change the water. Ducks will make a pond or any sitting water dirty in virtually no time. By having a small container you'll be able to change the water regularly and help to ensure no bugs and bacteria harm your ducks.

The size of the container is important. A duck needs to submerge its entire head. This allows them to clean their mucous membranes and keep them moist. They will also drink the water to wash dirty food down and use it to clean their mouth.

Providing they have clean water available every day your duck should be able to keep itself clean and pest free.

The best option is to find a plastic water tub or even a hard paddling pool. This can be filled, cleaned and refilled on a daily basis giving your ducks everything they need to be clean and happy. It can also be moved round their pen to help protect the ground!

A happy duck is more likely to lay eggs!

If you choose to put in a pond then it is advisable to use a readymade mold and ensure there is a drain on the bottom connected to a pipe that will take the water away from the duck pen. This will help you to keep the water clean.

The Pen

Now that you have chosen your ducks and the best way of giving them access to water you need to create a pen for them. This is how you will keep them safe from predators and allow them to enjoy their lives.

It is a good idea to cover the pen in case any of your ducks feel like trying to fly out.

You'll need several things to create the perfect pen:

- **Wire fencing**

- **Posts**

- **Wood**

- **Concrete**

- **Straw**

- **Tools**

The fencing is essential to surround the area that you have given to your ducks. This contains them and keeps the largest of prey out. Of course you need to use plenty of wood posts to ensure the fencing is secure.

But don't forget to leave a gap where you'll fit the wire fenced gate; you need to get into the pen!

Ideally you should bed the fencing into the ground; this will make it harder for predators to dig under the fencing and up into the pen. You can also put stones round the outside of the fence to help dissuade these animals.

Inside you'll need to decide where the water container is going and where their house will be. The house is essential as you must shut your ducks away at night; this will keep them safe.

The ideal duck house should be placed on a concrete base. This means that no predator can dig under and come up in their house. This will also allow you to build their house at ground level.

You may be tempted to build it on stilts to protect from predators. However, in reality this simply makes it more difficult for the ducks to go in and out; they won't be keen on using it.

Once you have a concrete pad then you can create any size house you wish. Obviously you need to consider how much room each duck will need to sleep and move round at night.

It is not generally worth putting in nest boxes for ducks; they will usually create their own nest of straw and you can collect the eggs from there.

This means that you must be able to get into the duck house to collect the eggs; a hatch is sufficient you don't need to make it tall enough for you to get in!

The roof will need to be covered to ensure the house is waterproof. You can use tarpaulin or roofing felt, whichever is within your budget.

The house itself can be made from wood bought at the local store or you could use pallets which can be picked up for free.

Your ducks will appreciate windows for when they are inside during the day. But, you need to have shutters that cover the windows at night; this prevents the predators from scaring them.

You should also have two entrances for your ducks which will allow two ducks to go through each entranceway at the same time; ducks can be pushy!

It is also important to consider the latches you use, especially if you are in an area that is home to raccoons. Raccoons are very clever and can operate some latches. It is said they can do the same sorts of things as a toddler so if you're toddler can get in so can a raccoon!

There is no correct design for your duck house. It just needs to be secure and dry; you can choose the shape.

Landscaping

Just because you are keeping ducks it does not mean that you need to have a barren area of land where they have picked all the grass and plants clean.

With a little effort you can landscape the area making it a more natural habitat for the ducks and nicer for you and your neighbors to look at.

Try doing this:

- **Add shrubs**

A ring of shrubs round your fencing will make the pen less visible to you and any predators. It will also make the ducks feel safer. As the shrubs are outside the pen there is little potential for the ducks to damage them.

Inside the pen you should also add a selection of shrubs. Butterfly bushes, rose bushes, hawthorn and juniper are all good choices.

When you first plant them you'll need to surround their base with stones; this will stop the ducks from pulling the roots out while looking for food.

If you wish you can even surround each shrub with wire fencing to enable it to become established. The ducks can then eat the leaves without destroying the plant.

Another good idea is to build garden boxes. These do not need to be tall but they do need a wire mesh top. You can then plant grass in the box and the ducks can eat it as it sticks out the top. This will again prevent them from damaging roots and allow the grass to keep growing; and feeding them.

You may also wish to add a few firs; these offer shade and most ducks are not interested in eating them. They can provide an attractive view from your neighbor's house instead of the duck pen.

Providing you protect the roots and the core of each plant anything can be planted n your duck pen; just be sure to verify that it is not dangerous to your ducks first.

Chapter 2 – Feeding And Caring For Your Ducks

Now that you have got your ducks and built them a beautiful pen you need to think about their food and how to look after them properly.

Remember, a happy duck is more likely to lay eggs!

Your ducks will forage round their pen, eating insects, berries from your plants and munching on the green leaves and grass.

This is good and is natural but you must ensure they get all the nutrition they need. This will help them to be healthy and produce eggs.

Duck Feed

Assuming you're interested in getting your ducks to lay eggs then you need to provide your ducks with feed daily. You should look for feed which is approximately 17% protein and high in calcium.

If you have ducklings then the feed will need to be closer to 20% protein but you also need to ensure the food pellets are small enough for the ducklings to eat without choking.

Grit

It is important that ducks are allowed to eat grit. This helps in the formation of egg shells and in keeping their digestive system working properly. If there is grit in their pen then you don't need to do anything else. If not you should add some to their food at least once a week.

Treats

Ducks love carrots, greens and corn but they are not necessarily very nutritious for them. Treats like these should be given in moderation. This will help to make sure your ducks are eating nutritionally good food and the treats are just extra.

Oyster Shells

This works for chickens and ducks. If you notice that the egg shells are pitted or very thin then you can a little oyster shells to their diet. This will improve the quality of the egg shells.

However, if you don't have ducks that lay eggs you should not give them oyster shells; it can be toxic.

It is worth purchasing small amounts of feed on a regular basis rather than buying large bags. This is the best way to ensure the feed is fresh.

Food which has been stored is likely to become damp and start to go moldy. This is especially true if the food is stored in a metal container where it can sweat.

Moldy food attracts bacteria which can be harmful to your ducks. It is definitely better to play safe than to watch your ducks get sick.

Top Tip:

Your ducks need to have water when they eat, this allows them to swallow their food and clean their mouths.

It is a good idea to keep their food a good distance away from their 'pond' and have a large bowl of water next to it.

This will help to reduce the risk of bacterial contamination in the bathing water.

You should also change the water daily and discard any food that has not been eaten at the end of the day. You'll soon get to know the right amount to put in for your ducks.

Taking Care Of Duck Health

Ducks are surprisingly tough creatures. But that doesn't mean they are invincible. The best approach is to visually inspect them all in the morning and the evening.

This will allow you to spot small changes and get them looked at before they become a bigger issue. You should also ensure you handle the ducks as this will help to keep them good natured.

As well as ruffling their feathers you need to look for parasites on their skin, abnormal droppings, a loss of appetite or an inability to stand properly.

If your duck has hurt itself or is becoming sick you're going to need to contact your veterinarian and decide what action to take.

Because ducks spend much of their time in the water they are generally parasite free. But, the following are common conditions in ducks kept as pets:

- **Angel Wing**

If your duck has a wing which seems incapable of lying flat against their body then there is a good chance they have angel wing.

This is not a life threatening condition. It is caused by a diet that is too high in protein. Switch to a lower protein diet and it will stop growing so fast. A sling can also help; if your duck will allow it.

- **Bound Crop**

If you notice a duck has a hard or swollen neck then there is a good chance that I has bund crop. This is where long grass or another object has become lodged in the upper part of their digestive tract.

You can massage the throat to help break up the blockage and feed them a little vegetable oil on a daily basis. Eventually the lodged object should move down the digestive tract. If it doesn't; you'll need veterinary help.

- **Aspergillosis**

Your duck will develop heavy breathing with this condition. It will appear to be struggling for breath as a result of fungal spores in the respiratory tract.

This is usually a result of wet feed and damp bedding. Remove this immediately and make sure it is dry in the future. It should clear up in a few days by itself.

It is also worth looking at why the feed and bedding is wet. If there is a design issue with your duck house or the food is becoming damped while being stored you need to remedy the issue as quickly as possible.

- **Bumblefoot**

This is very common in all ducks. You will notice a swelling in your duck's foot and a black scab on the underside.

It is likely that your duck has cut their foot and it has become infected. You will need medication to kill the infection before it spreads through the duck.

- **Botulism**

If you don't keep the water clean in their pen then the ducks are likely to contract this bacteria; it thrives in dirty water.

The fact that a duck can make any pool of water dirty in just a few minutes illustrates why you need to change the water daily. Ducks put their whole body in the water, including their face. It is very easy for bacteria to spread and become an issue.

This is extremely dangerous as the bacteria can kill a duck very quickly.

- **Eye Infections**

This often occurs after your ducks have mated. The process is rough. A male duck will grab the female's neck temporarily blocking the sinuses.

This causes bubbling round the eyes and the potential for infection. It can usually be treated with salt water rinse at least twice a day. You'll also need to change the water and the bedding even more frequently.

- **Egg Binding**

Sometimes a duck is unable to pass an egg; it gets stuck in the tube. The duck will make a lot of noise as this is a painful condition.

Soaking the duck in a warm bath and using vegetable oil round the tube exit should help to free the egg. If you can't get the egg to come out by itself then you may need help from your vet. Leaving it is not an option as it will cause additional health problems for your bird. It can even create an infection which could potentially kill your beloved pet.

24

Fortunately caring for your duck is easy, keep their pen clean and their water fresh and you'll dramatically reduce the likelihood of any of these illnesses.

Chapter 3 – Things To Avoid When Caring For Ducks

You can make your life much easier if you are aware of the biggest risk factors and what your ducks should avoid. This can prevent them from becoming ill and giving you an expensive vet's bill.

Here are some things that you should avoid when looking after your ducks:

Citrus Fruit

Citrus fruit has a direct affect on your duck's ability to absorb calcium. It reduces it! This means that your ducks bones can become weaker and their eggs shells will become thin.

Spinach works on their internal systems in the same way; avoid it.

Iceberg Lettuce

This green vegetable is generally good for you but only good for ducks in very small quantities.

It can cause diarrhea in your duck which will disturb their normal metabolism. This can result in low egg production or even a weakened immune system; allowing them to get ill.

Dried Beans

Fresh food always works best for your ducks. Dried beans are actually toxic to a duck! Only ever give them beans which are fresh and have sprouted.

Bread

You go to the park and feed the ducks bread, so you're going to do it at home too.

However, you may be surprised to find that bread is actually bad for ducks. Consumption of bread in ducks has been linked with obesity and a lack of proper nutrition.

Feeding them too much can also stop them from foraging for their own food; which is an essential survival trait all ducks should retain.

Limiting Food

If you've had chickens before you may be surprised at just how much ducks eat; it is significantly more than your average chicken.

It is important to make sure they always have fresh food available to meet their dietary needs. Remember, a happy duck is going to give you more eggs.

Their Droppings

Ducks quite often have salmonella germs in their droppings. These germs may not affect the duck but they can quickly get everywhere. Your ducks will walk through the droppings and then spread the germs across the bedding, the enclosure walls and everywhere else in their pen.

You can then pick up these germs on your hands, clothes and shoes. The germs are then transferred with you and, if you don't wash your hands can come into contact with your mouth, making you ill.

This is why it is essential to wash your hands after very visit to the duck pen. You must also ensure your children do the same thing.

Lack Of Ventilation

Many duck owners do not appreciate how much moisture a duck will breathe out. This can cause a problem in your duck house of you have not provided adequate ventilation.

Your duck house should have ventilation in the form of grills or even chicken wire at the top of it. The gap must be small enough to ensure predators cannot get in. There should be enough ventilation that the moisture from the ducks is allowed to escape.

If there isn't the inside of the duck house will become damp, allowing mold to grow. This will then cause your ducks to become ill.

Ignoring The Power Of Flight

Most ducks are simply too heavy to fly any distance. This is not true for the mallard which is an excellent flyer.

However, just because your duck shouldn't be able to fly don't underestimate its ability. It may still escape the pen. This is why you'll need to make a decision on whether to cover the roof of the pen with a fine wire mesh.

The sunlight will still get in but your ducks will be unable to leave. This can also give them extra protection from airborne predators.

It is worth noting that ducks are a tasty meal for hawks and other large birds; they have very little natural protection. If you keep them in an open pen with little shade or places to hide there is a very good chance that you'll lose at least one of them to a hawk.

However, you may feel that it is unfair to keep the duck contained. Giving them their freedom may mean that they do not return, although mallards are generally very good at returning to the same spot.

Less Is Not More!

Ducks are extremely social creatures. If you only have one or two they are likely to feel lonely and become depressed. You're unlikely to get any eggs and your duck may even die as it will not have any interest in food.

Equally you must be aware that a duck will relieve themselves roughly every 30 minutes. This means they are leaving a trail of droppings behind them. This is not just confined to their pen; they will do it in the duck house as well.

You must be prepared to clean up this mess in order for the ducks to remain healthy. In the wild it's not an issue as they cover a large area, your pen is likely to be more restrictive.

They Eat Everything

Whether you leave a bell lying round, decorative stones or several candies; your ducks will try to eat them. Foreign objects can cause choking and other issues inside their bodies.

You need to constantly be vigilant that the enclosure is safe for them.

Not Handling Them

Ducks are generally very friendly. However, male ducks can be territorial and if you don't handle them regularly they will often become aggressive if you then step into their territory. This can become an issue if you need to feed them and keep the area clean.

A duck bite is painful and likely to leave a bruise.

This is why it is important that you handle them regularly and find someone who will take proper care of them if you need to go away.

You may also find that many vets are not used to dealing with ducks which can make it more difficult for them to handle and treat them successfully.

Sexing And Aging

It is very difficult to work out which sew a duckling is. This means you are unlikely to get a male and female duckling as you hoped. You need to be prepared for this and for the fact that a duck is a long term commitment. They can live to be as old as 20!

Separate The Chickens

Chickens and ducks seem to have a lot in common. You may be tempted to keep the two types of birds together. However, did you know that a rooster will attempt to mate with a duck? Equally a drake will try to mate with a chicken hen!

This means if you have male ducks or chickens you can't mix them together, but females of the two species will get along just fine.

Overbuilding

Ducks do not need an elaborate duck house. They are extremely hardy creatures, much tougher than chickens. While your chicken needs to be fully enclosed at night the duck shelter can allow a breeze and some moisture in.

Do not try to make it airtight! You simply need to focus on keeping potential predators out; assuming they can make it into the fenced section first.

The Taste Of Duck Eggs

Duck eggs are generally larger than chicken eggs. If you overcook them they will go rubbery and they have higher levels of protein and fat.

This can all be considered positive. However, if you do have ducks in order to enjoy their eggs it is a good idea to verify that you like duck eggs first.

The eggs you collect from your ducks will be much stronger in taste than chicken eggs. This is fine for most people but if you don't like the flavor you will struggle to use the eggs; cooking does not ask the taste.

You'll have to be prepared to enjoy duck eggs or modify all your recipes to ensure they are palatable. Alternatively you could just avoid keeping the ducks!

Conclusion

There are many reasons why you may consider getting ducks instead of chickens or even as well as your chickens.

They are certainly friendly birds and can be a lot of fun to look after.

However, before you start it is important to be aware of the responsibility that comes with looking after ducks and what you should and shouldn't be doing.

The key points to take away are that any shelter will do for a duck; they prefer a bit of a breeze and some moisture. But, the shelter must be built well enough to keep predators out. Ducks have a lot of predators.

This is made more complicated by the fact that the shelter should be at ground level or very close. A duck will not enter a high shelter as it will be scared! Perhaps this is linked with the fact that most ducks are unable to fly.

It is also essential to provide water; both for drinking and swimming in. But, you don't need to build a big pond. Providing your ducks can swim round in a circle they will be happy to do so for most of the day.

There are many different types of duck; you need to choose the one that is best suited to your needs and that you can care for appropriately. Getting fresh eggs everyday is great but when there are just two humans and 4 ducks giving you up to 800 eggs a year; you will need to consider what else you can do with the eggs.

Either that or you may end up looking like a duck egg!

It can be a lot of fun looking after and playing with ducks. However it is also a long term commitment which is why it's essential that you know how to feed and care for your ducks before you get them. This guide should have helped you to create the right habitat for your ducks which will ensure they are happy and safe.

But, don't forget that even the quietest of ducks will make some noise and they are generally early risers. If you have immediate neighbors you must consider them. It is also worth checking with your local planning to ensure you are allowed to keep ducks and how many is the maximum.

Made in the USA
Middletown, DE
11 October 2020